I0101667

REJECTION
The Perfect Path to Perfection

A Treatise

CHARLES MWEWA

Copyright © 2024 Charles Mwewa

www.charlesmwewa.com

Published by:

ACP

Ottawa, ON Canada

www.acpress.ca

www.springopus.com

Email:

info@acpress.ca

All rights reserved.

ISBN: 978-1-998788-72-9

DEDICATION

To

all those who have suffered
from the pain of rejection.

CONTENTS

AUTHOR'S WORD

Rejection is more common than you think. At least every human being this author knows has been rejected at least twice in their lifetime. Some, even more than twice.

This author himself has been rejected several times. People erroneously think that rejection is always bad. Wrong. Rejection can be a plus, an asset.

Many good things have come from rejection. Some great leaders rose from the ashes of rejection. Some very successful businesspeople survived rejection.

Some innovations and inventions passed thorough the kiln of rejection. Rejection may come to anyone, but it matters how they treat their rejection.

This book shows you how to bounce from rejection.

1 | DEALING WITH REJECTION

Zones of Rejection

To reject is to spurn (slight, scorn, disdain, hold in contempt, or disregard) a person's affections. People can and are rejected in relationships, including divorce. They are rejected in job interviews. They are rejected in competitive games. They are rejected in assessments, business, academia, court (losing a case), etc. As you read this, you might be a victim of rejection even in an area not mentioned here.

Feelings of Rejection

The feeling of rejection is real. There is no human being who does not feel the pain of rejection. However, some receive it with hardship than others. The central truth is that every human being feels the pangs of rejection in some degree.

The Pain of Rejection and Its Manifestation

People deal with the pain of rejection in different ways. Some are destroyed, even permanently so, by it. Others take longer to recover. Some become prisoners of the rejection. Others learn from it and move on. But everyone reacts in some way to rejection.

Rejection can destroy many things. It can kill self-esteem. It can maim confidence. It can frustrate dreams, visions and potentials. It can cause mental and psychological problems and disorders. It can even kill physically (such as through suicide, etc.).

Reasons for Rejection

People can be rejected for many reasons. And, of course, and honestly, this is what people fear most about rejection. The reason or reasons for rejection are, sometimes, more painful than the rejection itself. Reasons can range from lack of performance to failure to deliver; not being able to meet the standard to over-qualification; lacking in a critical characteristic to inborn or innate disadvantage; losing favor to over-ambition; because one is violent to one is a saint; discovery of better and loftier goals to loss of vitality, drive or abilities.

Some reasons may include nothing changing in a long or short time to something changing very radically and quickly. Others include: A mistake was made to no progress was sustained; greed to foolishness; value lost to value gained; weight to height; dark to light and vice versa; perceived ugliness to perceived beauty; employment to unemployment; educated to uneducated; high status in life to low status in life; tribe to culture and everything in between; color of skin to national origin; having children to lack of children; richness to poverty, etc. The list is inexhaustible. But for whatever the reason, the pain is the same.

The reason for rejection brings enormous and excruciating feelings of "defeat." This feeling has led to more misery than the experience of rejection itself. It can be very "paralyzing," when someone (the subject or victim) feels immobilized and mentally or physically incapable. This feeling is real, and if not treated or if treated poorly, it may lead to worse experiences than rejection.

Some people have lost the will to live, and others have been made to give up easily on other aspirations. People who feel a sense of rejection do not feel like trying – they may give up hope altogether.

There is an assumption that the manner of receiving rejection impacts the recipient adversely or mildly. That is only by some degree. All rejections, given gently or maliciously, induce feelings of failure. Employers may begin the salutations by appealing to the sense of effort made, but once they mention the verdict (the indictment), the recipient may still feel a sense of immobilization. However, it is better to be more sensitive and civilized in discharging a rejection than being careless and malicious.

Human resource departments in places of employment are now learning that the way a rejection is communicated to the recipient is more important than the rejection itself.

It is, though, worse to keep silent than to release a rejection. People who are rejected must be told of the rejection. Whether it is in judicial decisions, political election results or in announcing a divorce or a loss of something or someone, or in bidding for commodities or in competitive games, people have a right to know that they have been rejected.

The important thing to bear in my mind is that the manner in which the rejection is handed out can heal or kill. Behaviors and words like, "You're fired," "We or I don't want or like you," "You're useless," or "Leave!" do not only lack the taste, but they can be lethal to the recipient. They may lead to suicidal ideations or even to suicide. People have value, even if they may be rejected momentarily. Because of this innate, inherent value all human beings have, the communication of a rejection must be handled with absolute care, sensitivity and reasonableness.

2 | STEPS IN DEALING WITH REJECTION

Acknowledgment

First, acknowledge that you have been rejected. Do not dance around it. Be bold and humble enough to admit defeat, however bitter or painful it might be at the time. Say loudly to yourself (even multiple times), "I have been rejected."

Acknowledging that one has been rejected provides a quick but effective closure. Denial does not close the case; it merely sustains and prolongs the pain. No matter how painful pain is, it expiates. Pain does not last forever. Even if it persists, it may be dislodged by death. But denial prolongs pain beyond what is reasonable.

Acceptance

Second, accept the rejection. This is the phase which is very difficult to navigate. Many people are not only deniers, but they refuse to accept that they have been rejected. It seems to make sense to simply say that one is not rejected, or that maybe there is only a misunderstanding, or that the giver of the rejection will rescind it in time, but all such strategies are futile.

Many people refuse to accept that they have been rejected because it could hurt their pride. Some people believe that they are perfect, and that no human being can ever reject them.

This may happen to people who have been praised, fluttered or "worshipped" since they were little. It may happen to those who believe that they are intelligent, smart, accomplished, beautiful, handsome, gifted, or idolized. This category of people is framed in the mentality of perfection, invincibility, faultlessness, etc. People in this branch of thinking may believe that no-one is better than them.

That is not only wrong, it is a fallacy. Sometimes even the best is rejected, and this can be for many reasons. It may not mean that someone does not acknowledge their accomplished nature or skillset or brilliance, it could be that they are feared, or they stand a better chance to succeed or similar-situated motivations. Rejection is not always for unpalatable motivations; sometimes, it is about the opposite. However, no matter the motivation, rejection is painful.

Accepting that one has been rejected, immobilizes the rejection and depletes it of its power to hurt. It sounds contrary to our mental cognition. But it is the truth. Not accepting a rejection harms; accepting it releases. Pain, eventually, dwindles and vanishes. Not accepting a rejection behaves, for the most part, like unforgiveness. The one who rejected (subject) might have gone and is busy being preoccupied with new ventures. However, the one who was rejected (object), may continue to be haunted and harmed by the rejection.

If one has to win over rejection, they must accept it soon as they acknowledge it.

Atonement

Third, atone for the rejection. Atonement is an ancient practice of paying for one's faults. It has been recognized as one of the best resolutions to conflicts. A version of it still persists in ecclesiastical and legal jurisdictions. Atonement is not a weakness; it is a strength.

Recompensing, penance and making amends may seem to be adverse actions to take for a victim of rejection, but they are greatly recommended. In reverse, it might seem reasonable for the perpetrator (the rejector) to atone for their rejecting. But the opposite is the case. The rejector holds no grudge. In fact, in rejecting, they might have been loosed or set free from their burden. The one who may hold a grudge is the rejected. And it is these who must expiate or atone for their sense of being rejected.

They must "give back" to the rejector, and hold nothing against the rejector. And this is an objective testimonial rather than a subjective one. The measures of one's expiation or atonement are in these: The ability to forgive; the ability to let go; the ceasing of pain when the rejector comes up; a willingness to deal with the rejector again in other forums or activities without feeling offended; if in matters of heart (such as marriage or relationships), the ability not to feel pain or bitter or jealous when the rejected meets or mentions the rejector or their new partners or endeavors; etc. Rule of thumb, atonement has taken place when the rejected is no longer beholden to the rejector, mentally, psychologically or otherwise. The rejected is free of the rejector.

Attornment

The fourth and last step in dealing with rejection is attornment. Attornment (and not atonement) is a legal term. It may mean the formal transference of something to someone else. It is commonly applicable to real estate transactions. In that area of law, it is defined as the act of granting authority or jurisdiction to a party even though no legal rights exist.

In actuality, attornment is akin to the biblical concept of grace. It makes one assume legal rights where none existed in the first place. In social or street parlance, it means to receive what one did not deserve.

When applied to rejection, the attornment stage or step allows the rejected to give back to the rejector, indirectly, by doing the following ten things (not an exhausted list).

Hold the rejector in high esteem. It may seem contradictory in terms, but treating the rejector better than they treated you is a plus. It might seem harder, and even atrocious, but it must be done. It will guarantee one absolute freedom.

Forgive the rejector unconditionally. Do not attach conditions, simply let go. It does not do you any good to continue to hold them tightly in your revenge chamber. Forgive them and forget.

Trade revenge for love or kindness or goodness. It is human to feel like revenging against those and interests we feel betrayed us. But to hold off revenge against our rejector is a benevolent act. No matter their motive, reason or interest in rejecting you, they are not worthy of your vengeance. Leave vengeance to chance and to God.

Be hopeful. No matter how painful, degrading or disheartening the rejection was, keep your spirits high. In majority of the cases, when you are rejected, you may end up gaining the best and the ideal. Some rejections are a blessing in disguise.

Thank the rejector for pointing out a defect or weakness or liability in you. You can always turn a liability into an asset. Think of the possibility that if you were not rejected, you might not have known that you had a weakness or blemish that needed fixing. Then consider evaluating the rejection and from it deriving lessons learned. Your next opportunity may end up being the best experience of your lifetime.

Use the rejection to forge a successful way forward. Some rejections are pointers to an ideal future. Some people who divorced ended up remarrying and bouncing. The newer partner might even have brought them the most lasting and satisfying relationship.

Some rejections are promotions in disguise. Imagine being rejected for a job that, unknowing to you and to them, was failing. You might just end up being employed by a stable employer. Sometimes, a rejection might have been a rescuer from danger or death. Some rejections may be answered prayers.

Use rejection as catalyst for something progressive. As an author one publisher's rejection of your manuscript might be a sign that it needed improvement. And by luck or diligence, after improving it, you might even end up courting a better publisher.

Bless the rejector and move on. Say something good about the rejector. And remember, it is wiser to not discuss the rejector's foibles than doing so as a way of getting at them. You may know the past and the present, but you do not know the future. There are cases were a former slave became a master, a boss a servant and a loser a winner.

And pray for, or wish, the rejector well in their future endeavors, or careers or business or relationships, whatever the case might be. Do not wait for them to fail so that you can say, "I knew it." That would simply vindicate your insecurity and sense of retaliation. It is not wise to wish your rejector the worst; it is better to wish them well. And, in fact, see them excel. That will bring you fortunes, if not if this present world, then in the one to come.

3 | TURNING REJECTION INTO PERFECTION

Rejection Viewpoint

Human stories are told from the failure, rejection and even desperation viewpoints. These are the stories that have made powerful movements, individuals, businesses, inventions, innovations, and great discoveries possible.

Acceptance is Risk

Although acceptance is a good feeling, it is, nevertheless, a risky feeling. Acceptance is every human's default position. There is an assumption of acceptance in life. Children expect their parents to accept them. Spouses expected to be accepted by their significant others. Relatives expect to accept one another. And nationals expect to accept each other. This is only upset by the feeling and experience and expectation to the contrary.

Acceptance is risk. Because when rejection comes, it devastates one in more ways than one. People who expect to be rejected, fare better than those who take it for granted that they would be accepted. The former have better defences than the latter.

Rejection as a Quality Control Mechanism

In industry, an entire department may be dedicated to quality control. An Online Dictionary defines quality assurance as a system of maintaining standards in manufactured products by testing a sample of the output against the specification. In manufacturing parlance, rejection is a welcome act; it propels the product towards continuous improvement. It may even prevent costly liabilities later on.

When a person is rejected, it may be painful, granted. But it may as well be a blessing in disguise. It could open up a whole new adventure or visioning. There are some politicians who are rejected in elections several times but end up being the best leaders by comparison after being elected. The previous rejections chiseled their previously unrefined potentials in leadership. Many successful businessmen and women were initially rejected. Many authors' original manuscripts were rejected. Many inventors' original patents or inventions were rejected. Even Jesus Christ was rejected.

What all these have in common is that they took advantage of their rejections and used such to their benefit. They did not dwell on what could-have-been, rather, they refocused their attentions and dreamed new dreams. They were unstoppable, and that is why they made it into the success book of records.

Rejection may be a door to continuous improvement.

Rejection as a Silent Motivator

Some people are extremely careful and do pay exceeding attention to details, because they were once rejected. Some discovered who they really were after being rejected. Others found new careers, new talents and even gathered new momentum for domination. The voice of rejection can be the loudest megaphone to progress. Excellence is only possible after rejection – because rejection demands exceptional treatment of future opportunities and chances.

Rejection as an Asset

Rejection is an asset when it can be a catalyst for change. The pain of rejection can foster resilience to other fears and pain. For example, someone who has been rejected before may not fear to make farther attempts. Those who have been rejected can bounce back. They can redeem themselves.

Rejection as Dearest Teacher

Some people are rude, they lack finesse, and may even mistreat servants and workers under them. They may even abuse trust and the necessary *bona fides*. That is, mostly, because they have never been rejected. Some people who have suffered from rejection may be the best teachers, leaders and instructors – because they do not want others to suffer from rejection.

People who have been rejected can use their experience to help others. They can mentor others and provide direction. They can laugh over their own experience of rejection and empower others to have resolve and not to be deterred by occasional rejections.

Rejection can be power.

ABOUT THE AUTHOR

Award-Winning, Best-Selling Author, Charles Mwewa (LLB; BA Law; BA Ed; LLM), is a prolific researcher, poet, novelist, lawyer, law professor and Christian apologist and intercessor. Mwewa has written no less than 100 books and counting in every genre and has exhibited his works at prestigious expos like the Ottawa International Book Expo and is the winner of the Coppa Awards for his signature publication, *Zambia: Struggles of My People*.
Mwewa and his family live in the Canadian Capital City of Ottawa.

SELECTED BOOKS BY THIS AUTHOR

1. *ZAMBIA: Struggles of My People (First and Second Editions)*
2. *10 FINANCIAL & WEALTH ATTITUDES TO AVOID*
3. *10 STRATEGIES TO DEFEAT STRESS AND DEPRESSION: Creating an Internal Safeguard against Stress and Depression*
4. *100+ REASONS TO READ BOOKS*
5. *A CASE FOR AFRICA?S LIBERTY: The Synergistic Transformation of Africa and the West into First-World Partnerships*
6. *DECOLONIZATION: Reclaiming African Originality and Destiny*
7. *A PANDEMIC POETRY, COVID-19*
8. *ALLERGIC TO CORRUPTION: The Legacy of President Michael Sata of Zambia*
9. *BOOK ABOUT SOMETHING: On Ultimate Purpose*
10. *CAMPAIGN FOR AFRICA: A Provocative Crusade for the Economic and Humanitarian Decolonization of Africa*
11. *CHAMPIONS: Application of Common Sense and Biblical Motifs to Succeed in Both Worlds*
12. *CORONAVIRUS PRAYERS*
13. *HH IS THE RIGHT MAN FOR ZAMBIA: And Other Acclaimed Articles on Zambia and Africa*
14. *I BOW: 3500 Prayer Lines of Inspiration & Intercession from the Heart: Volume One*
15. *INTERUNIVERSALISM IN A NUTSHELL: For Iranian Refugee Claimants*
16. *LAW & GRACE: An Expository Study in the Rudiments of Sin and Truth*
17. *LAWS OF INFLUENCE: 7even Lessons in*

INDEX

www.ingramcontent.com/pod-product-compliance
Lightning Source LLC
Chambersburg PA
CBHW060702280326
41933CB00012B/2274